Tomatoes Everywhere

Eduardo Aparicio

Contents

Rigby

A Harcourt Achieve Imprint

www.Rigby.com
1-800-531-5015

Do you like ketchup?
Do you like it on french fries?
Many people think ketchup
makes food taste good.
Did you know that ketchup is made
from tomatoes?

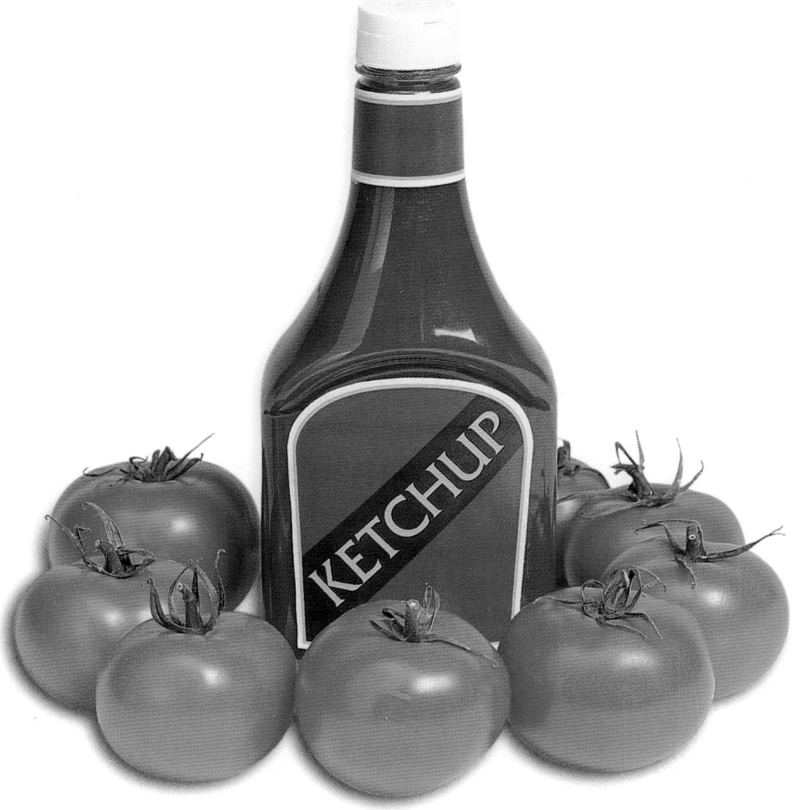
KETCHUP

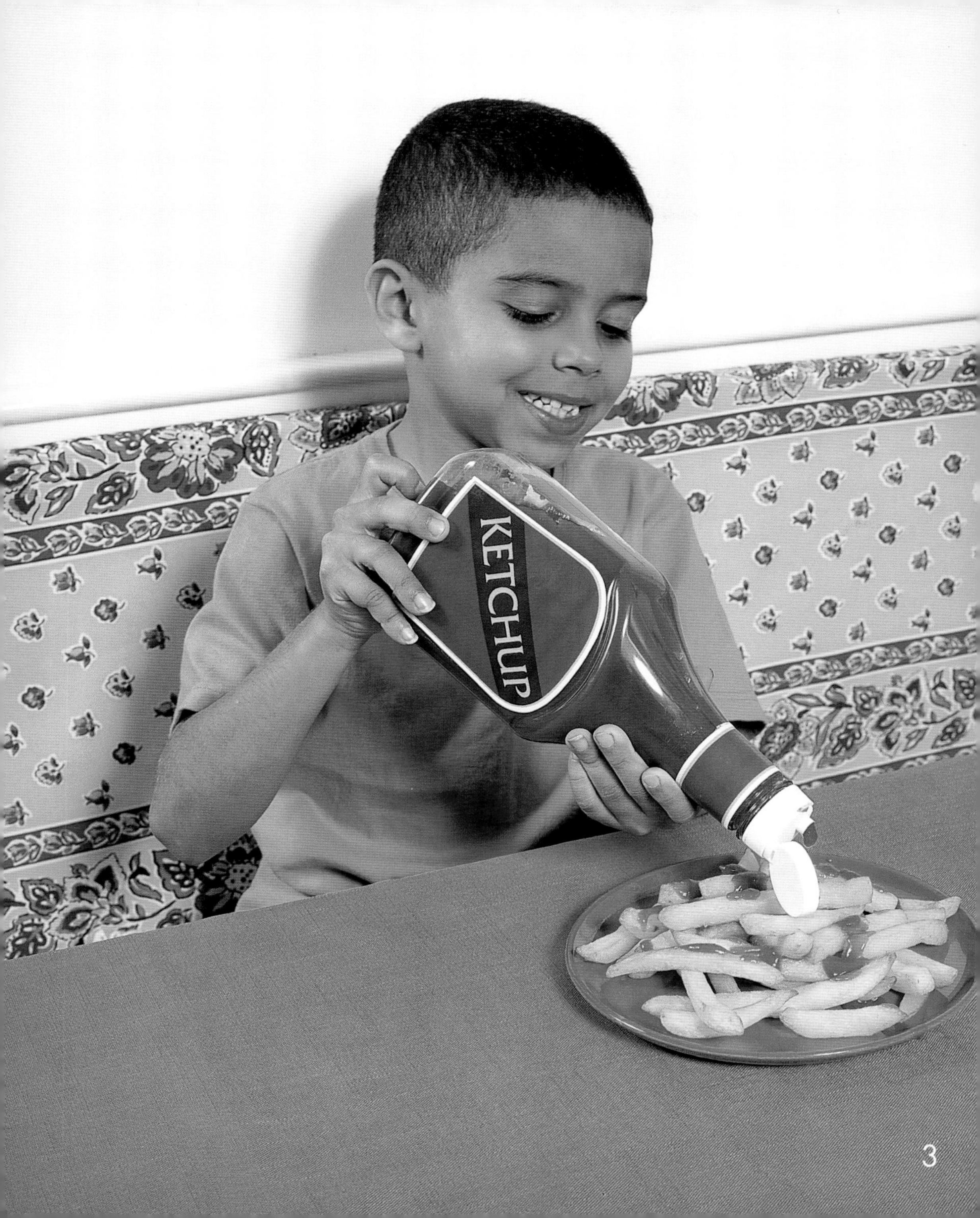
KETCHUP

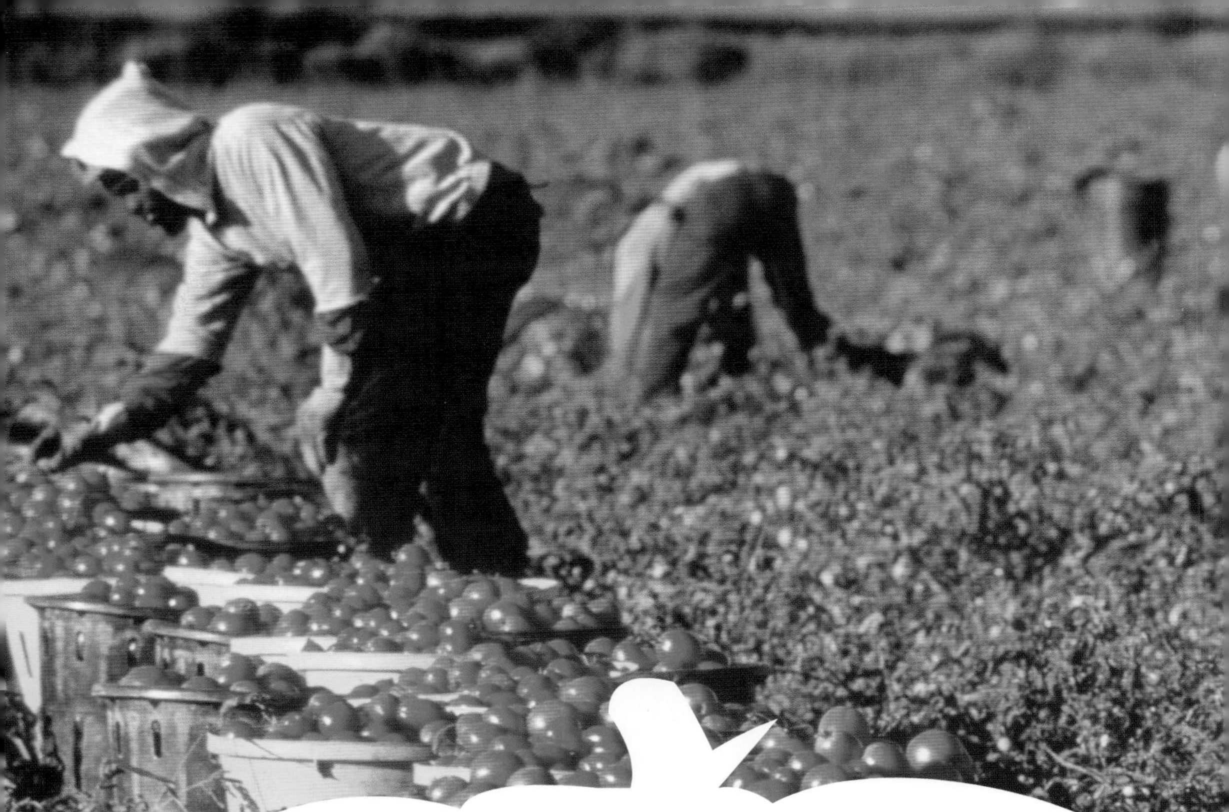

Tomatoes are fruits.
Tomatoes grow on plants.
Here you can see people
who are working on a tomato farm.
They are picking tomatoes.

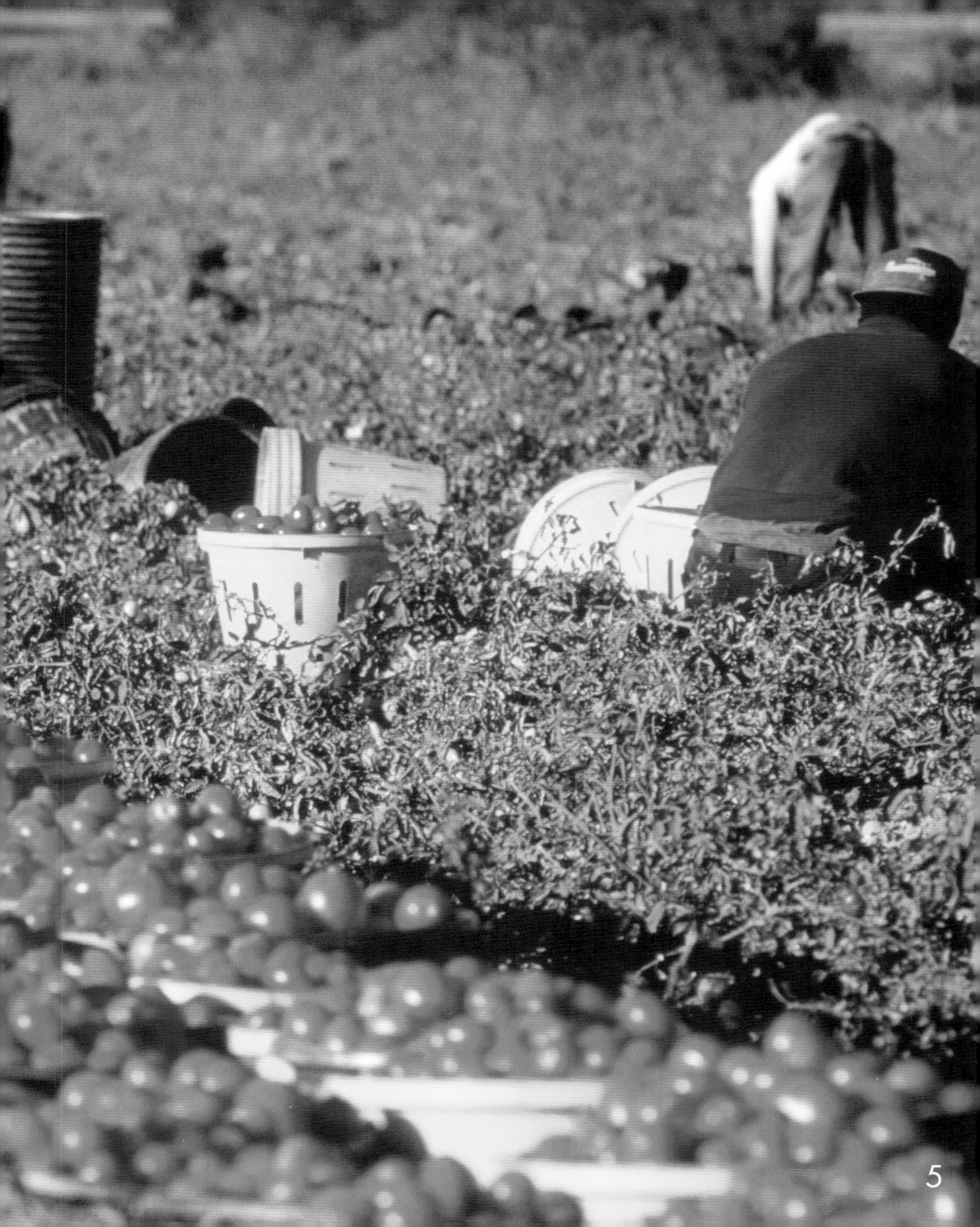

Tomato farms are not new.
People began to grow tomatoes
a long time ago.
People in Mexico and Peru
had tomato farms.

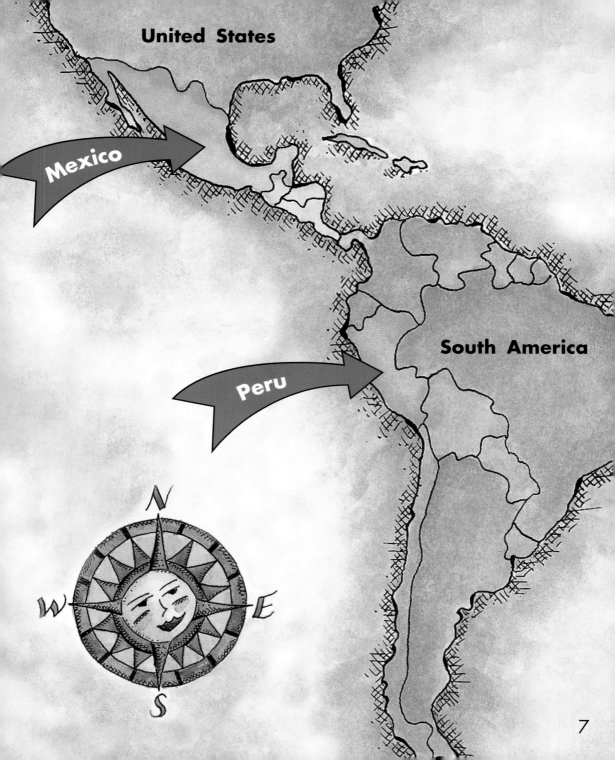

United States

Mexico

Peru

South America

N

W E

S

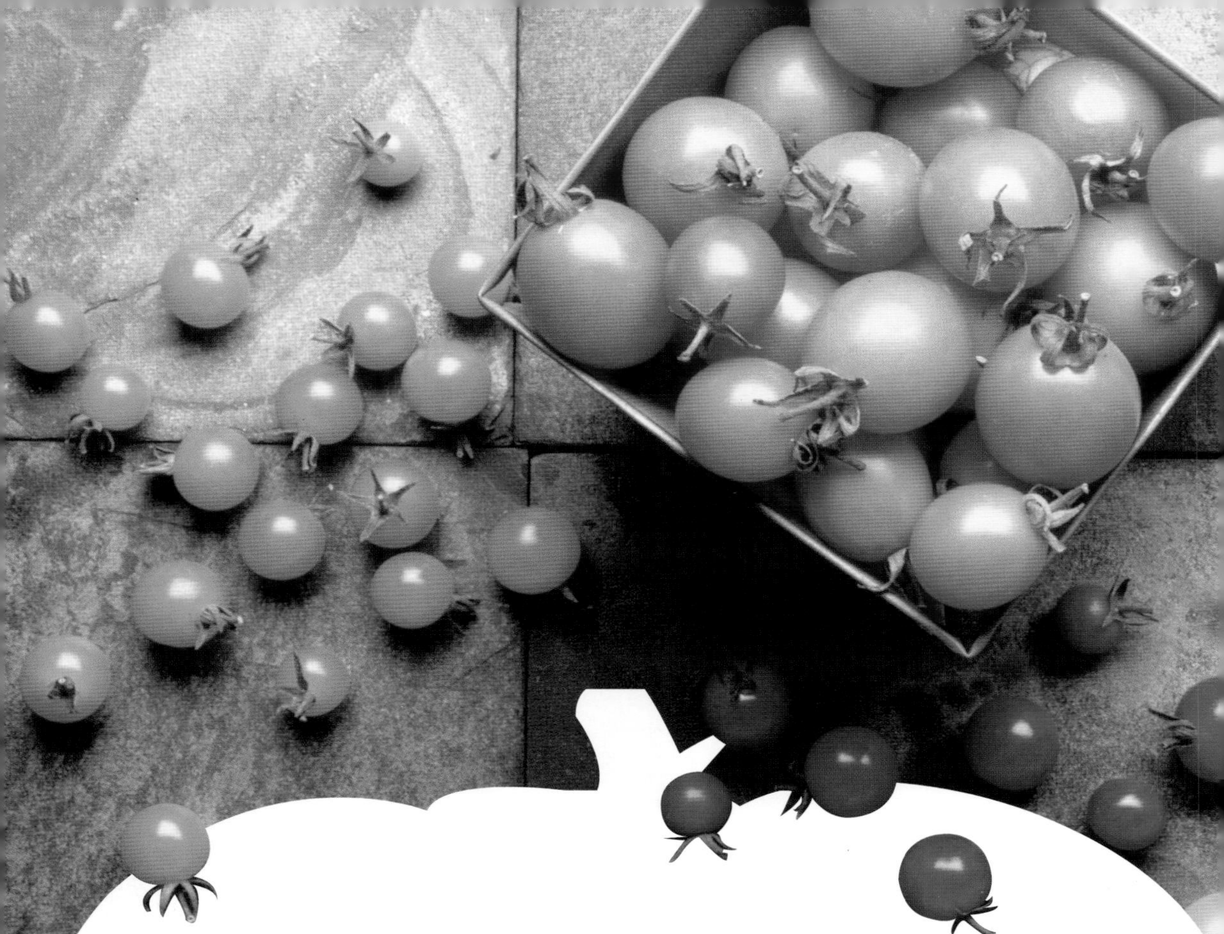

Today we have many kinds of tomatoes.
Some tomatoes are red, round, and big.
Some tomatoes are small and orange.
Some tomatoes are long and yellow.

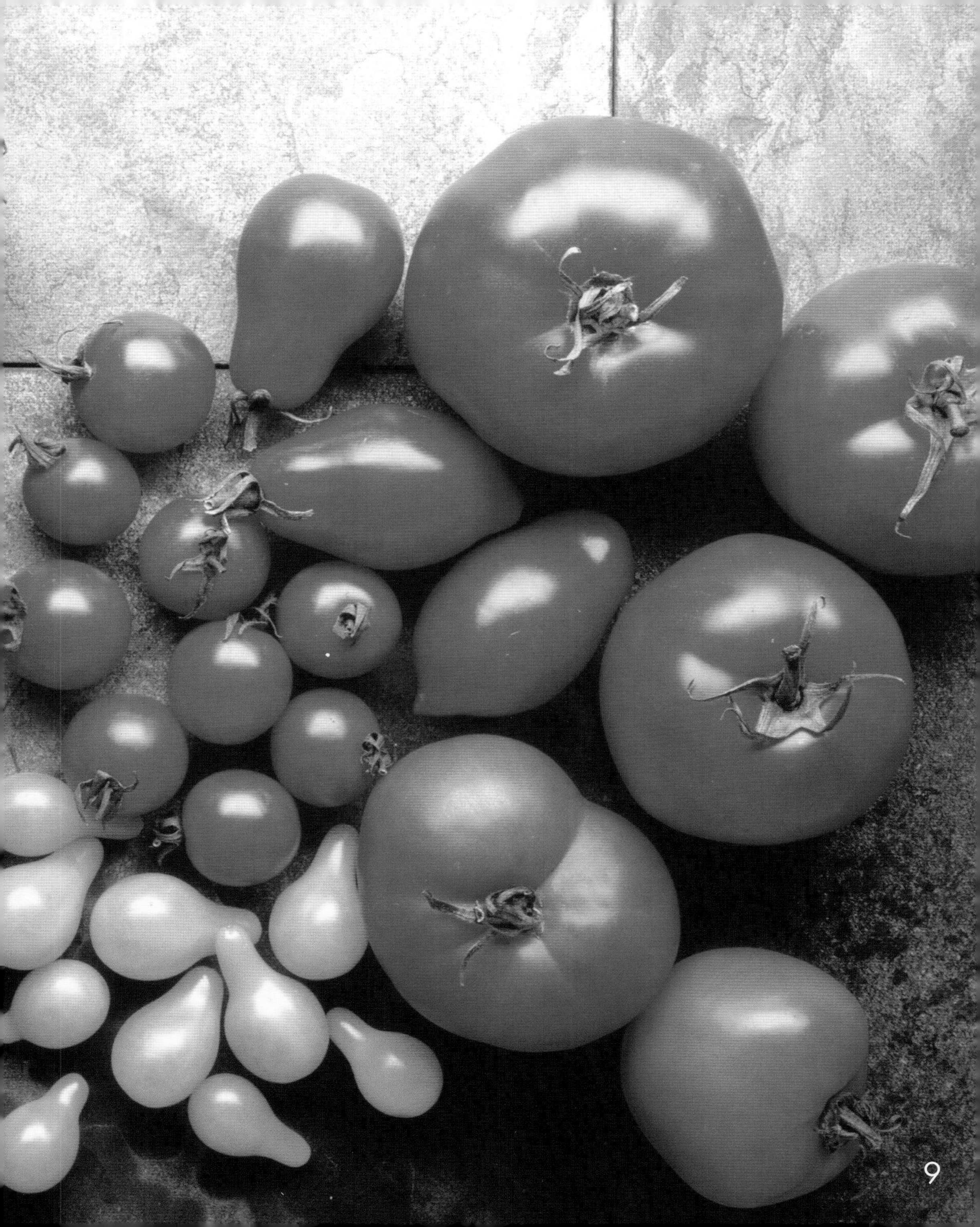

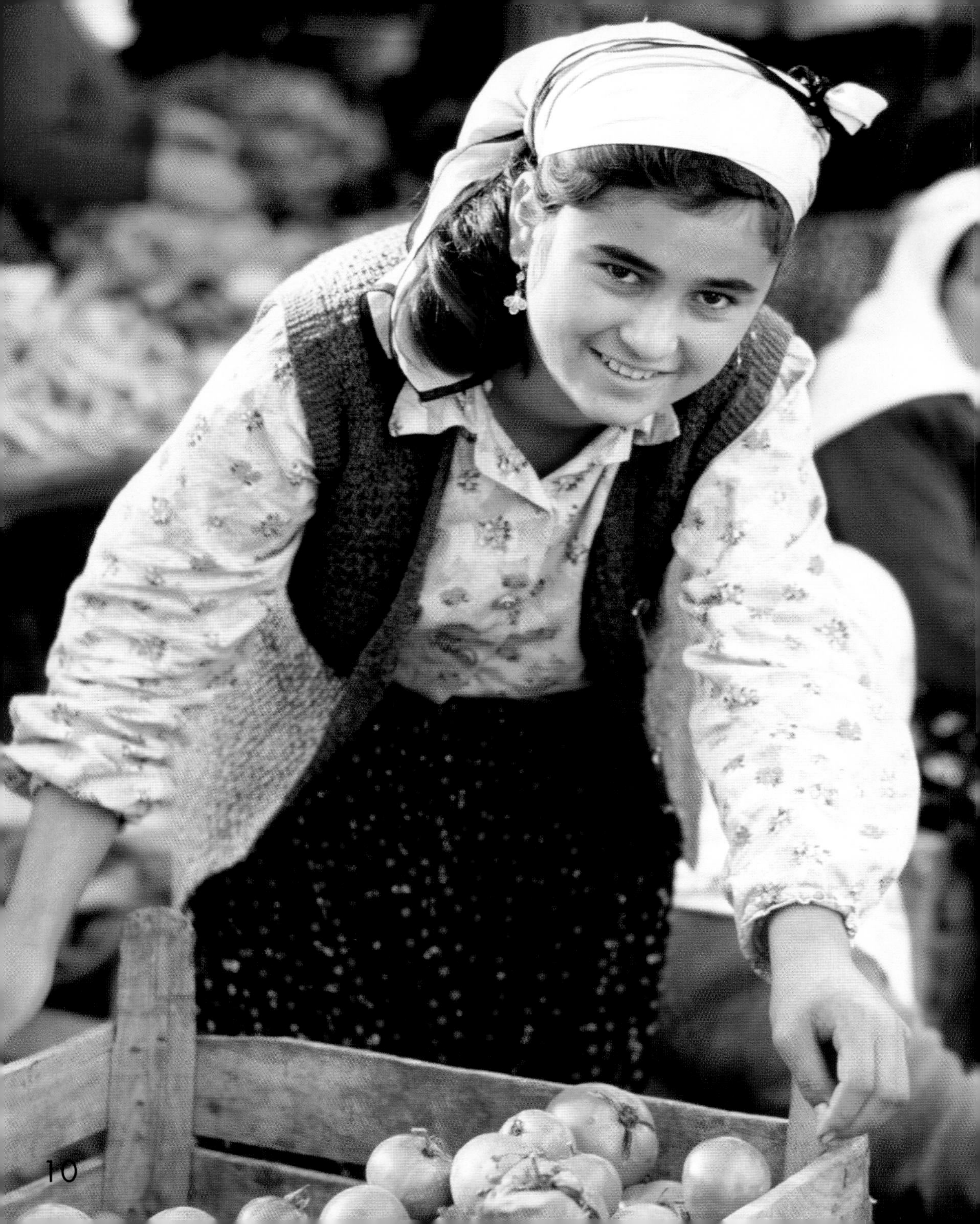

Workers on tomato farms
pack tomatoes in boxes.
Trucks bring the tomatoes
to the store.

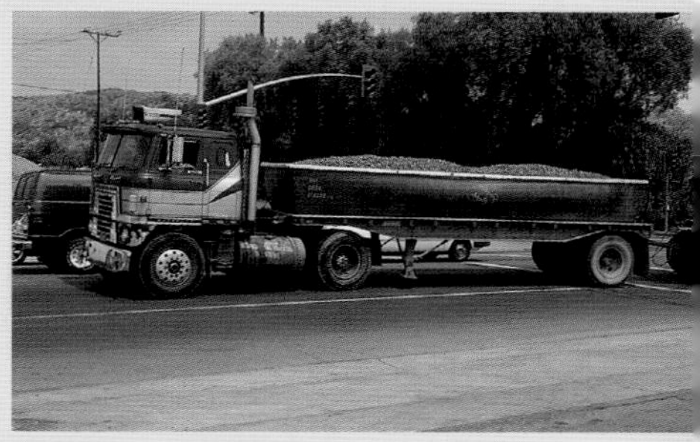

Then you can buy them!

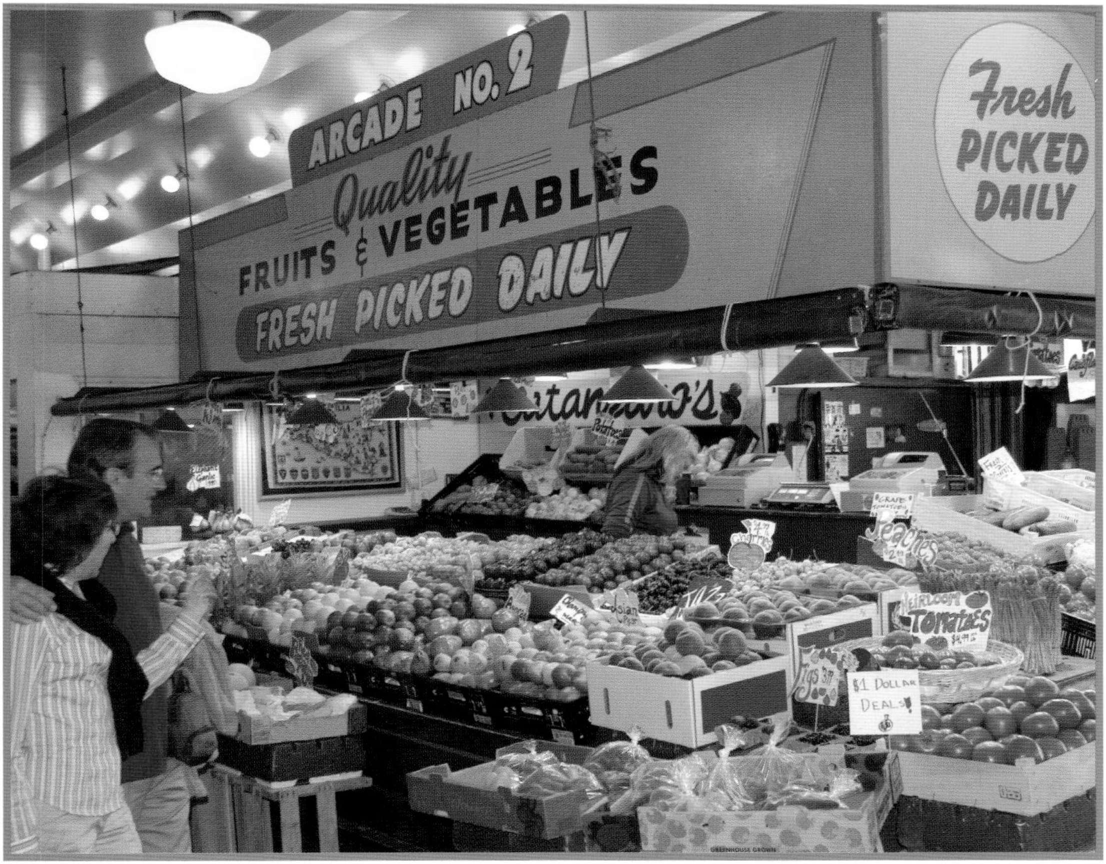
ARCADE NO. 2
Quality
FRUITS & VEGETABLES
FRESH PICKED DAILY
Fresh
PICKED
DAILY
$1 DOLLAR
DEALS!

People use tomatoes
to make tomato juice.
They put tomatoes in a big machine
that presses out juice.
Machines also make tomato sauce
for pizza and salsa for tacos.

TOMATO SAUCE
MEDIUM
MEDIUM
SALSA

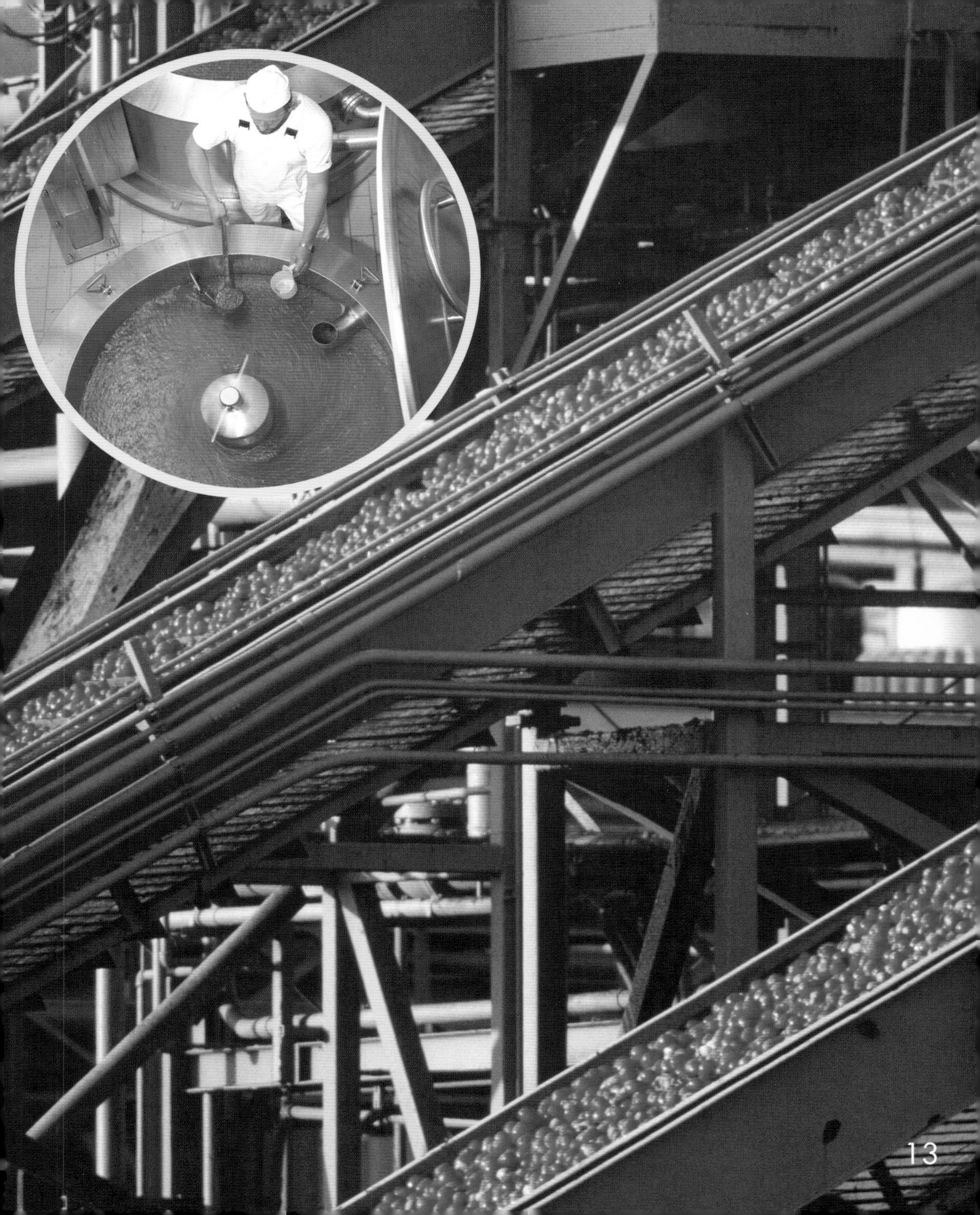

Making pizza is easy!

You need
- tomato sauce
- cut tomatoes
- cheese
- a flour tortilla

1. Put the tomato sauce on a tortilla.
2. Add the tomatoes and cheese on top.
3. Ask an adult to put the pizza in the oven at 350 degrees and bake it for 10 minutes.

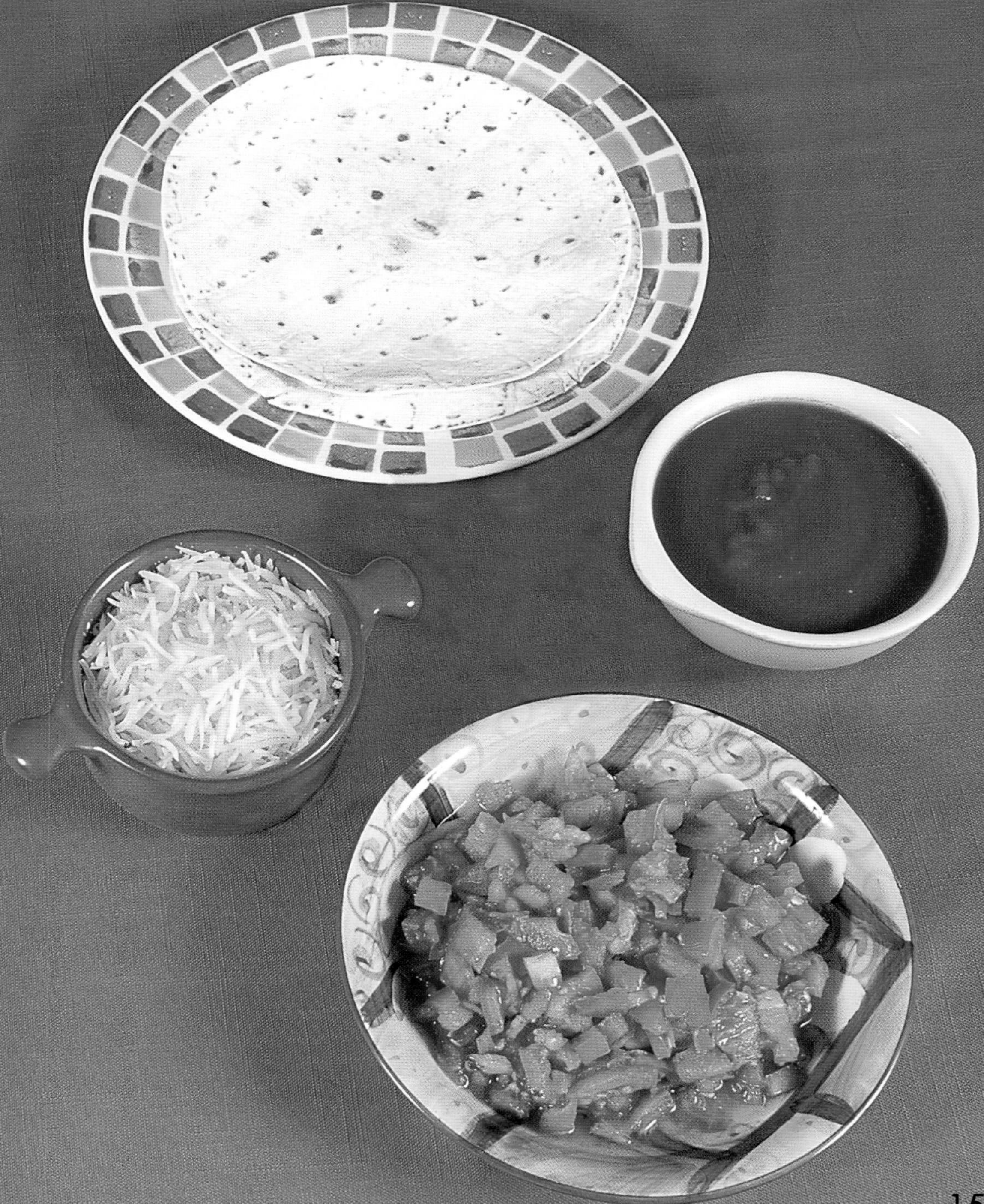

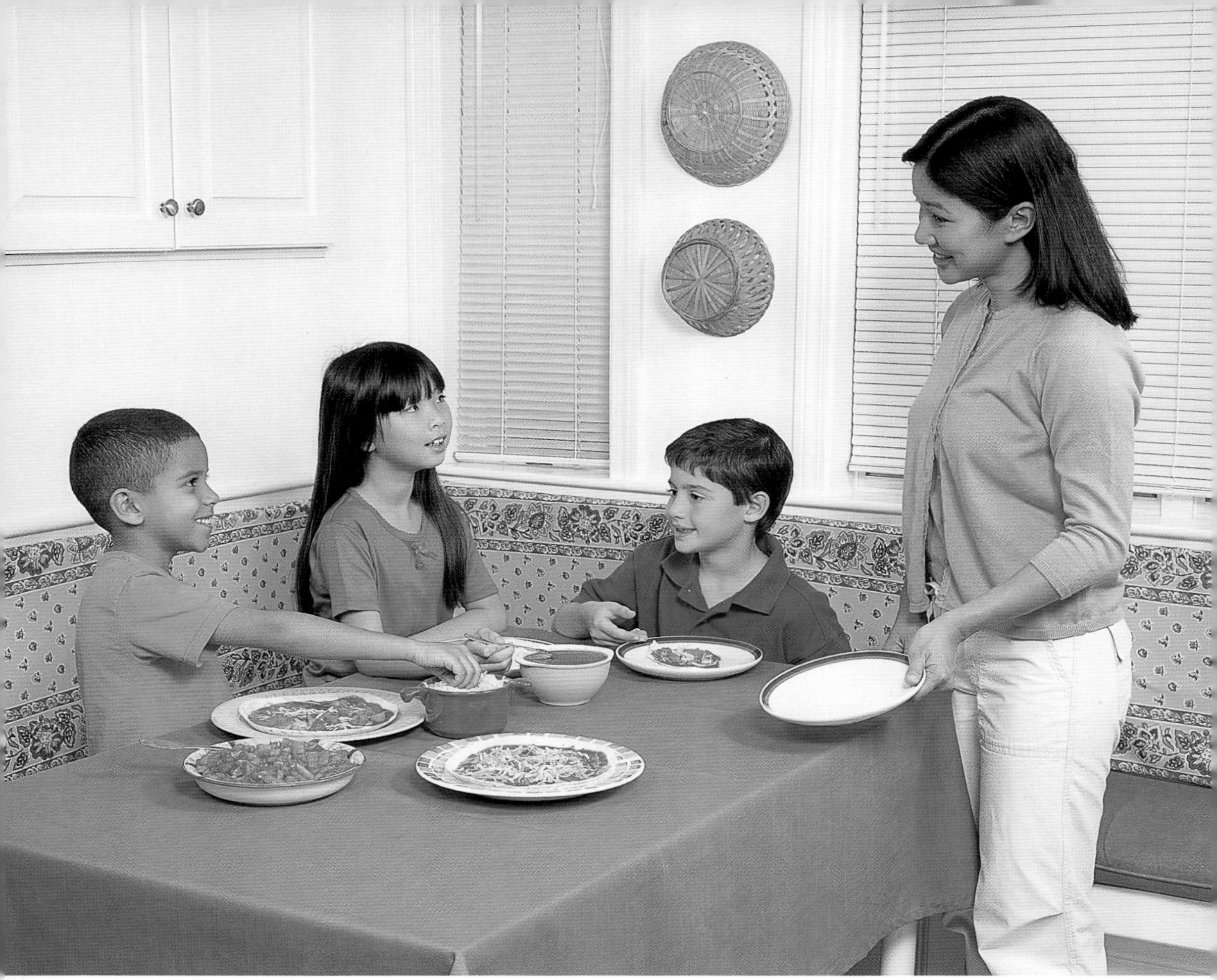

You can have
your own pizza party at home.
Your friends will love it!